I dedicate this book to the school of hard knocks and to my precious and supportive wife, Dee.

Make a Difference

Difference

in Your Life and Others

STEVE SCHIPPEL

Order this book online at www.trafford.com
or email orders@trafford.com

Most Trafford titles are also available at major online book retailers.

Print information available on the last page.

ISBN: 978-1-4907-7887-7 (sc)
ISBN: 978-1-4907-7888-4 (e)

Library of Congress Control Number: 2016919487

Trafford rev.   11/18/2016

 www.trafford.com
North America & international
toll-free: 1 888 232 4444 (USA & Canada)
fax: 812 355 4082

Contents

Contents

Introduction

If you have picked up this book to read and you are like many people who are working to become better at your career, better at your sport, or really at anything, then you have come to the right place. What is inside these pages will help you learn why many people, who work hard, have great dreams, a great desire to succeed, and are truly motivated, fail to accomplish what they want. Sometimes you might just fall a little short and sometimes you may fall way off track. You might even quit altogether. But if you turn that desire into a dream and then into a goal that you live and expand that desire into a Burning Desire, then you will become a Difference Maker.

It is my intent as you read through these pages and think about what you have done already, that you understand the additional steps it will take to build whatever you want for yourself. I firmly believe that if you become the best that you can be, then you and everyone around you will reap the benefits all of the hard work and effort you use to make your goals become dreams and then your dreams become reality.

There have been many books written about goal setting. Most of them by extremely successful speakers that travel the world helping people become motivated to go out there and get it done. I'm not one of those people who have made millions selling books or speaking to people. I am someone who has learned through listening, reading, and then taking action. I have accomplished more than most and sometimes even what others thought was impossible. Some of what I say I'm very confident that you have heard before. These thoughts I am about to share with you are not only what I have heard, but more importantly, took the action to make them into reality.

While taking action, I have experienced many insights that I truly believe will help you. Behind these ideas and thoughts are the remarkable feelings that form the foundation of turning dreams into reality. And I imagine that you have not heard or thought of these feelings in the same manner. It is putting all of this together that will be the difference – your difference. If you are working hard and you want to go to the next level of success, then truly take action on what I have recorded in this book. If you do, then you will become the best you can be and someone who is a Difference Maker.

Difference Makers Burn with Desire

Can you imagine having within you a goal which is so profoundly intense that it forces you to push yourself beyond the boundaries that you have lived within your entire life? Once you do this, then you have witnessed the Burning Desire necessary to achieve your goals. And when you live from your Burning Desire you will be able to be a difference maker.

I can help you take steps towards the dreams and goals you have always wanted. I know many of you have tried and tried again to set goals, then reset them, only to continue to fail. You become frustrated with the goal and then discontinue trying. You Give Up.

If you are able to examine your past and how you have developed to this point in your life, then you will be able to grow and actually change your current belief system, which in turn will help you stretch and become the best that you can be. It seems utterly ridiculous to some people that a Burning Desire needs to be explained at all. Then, there are those who do not have the slightest inkling of what it means to truly experience a Burning Desire.

So what is the nature of a Burning Desire? A Burning Desire is that moment when you sense a powerful feeling inside of you which screams that you NEED to accomplish a goal, that you NEED to have your goal, and that you NEED to do whatever it takes to reach your goal. Your need is so deeply intense that it actually hurts. It could be butterflies, an upset stomach, an ache in your heart, or any other feeling that tells you, "WOW! I really need this..." That is your Burning Desire.

Sometimes people mistake this feeling for anxiety and believe that perhaps their goal is simply too steep of a challenge or that perhaps it is too much of a stretch, but remember one statement that you will see repeated often in my writing: Napoleon Hill said, **"Whatever the mind can conceive and believe, it can achieve."**

Indeed, this means that your path could become a very difficult and rough road before you finally embrace the light at the end of the tunnel, but if the goal means something supremely important to you, if you really want to be a difference maker, then you will be able to find the strength and conviction to be able to give up a season for the rest of your life.

I will talk more about goals later, but for now let's say that your Burning Desire can be anything from a goal that is tangible such as a particularly beautiful car, a grandiose home that you passed by or walked through, or a fabulous piece of clothing that you would "die" for. I realize you might take that statement on face value and believe that there should not be any "tangible" goal that is worth that much. You have to understand that it is usually not the tangible goal which matters but rather the key is what that goal represents. I hope that you are able to fully understand what I mean by that statement. If you are reading this, hopefully you consider yourself an achiever and maybe even a high achiever and truly want to make a difference in your life and the world around you.

Personal Journey

Allow me to give you a little personal background. When it comes to taking action the best way I can share my thoughts and feelings is to share with you my life experiences.

2

I hope you can see yourself in my story. I have been fortunate to live a life full of experiences. Some are positive and some are not so positive. In fact, some are darn right negative no matter how much of a positive twist you want to put on them. I like to say that life will throw curve balls at us once in a while. At times we might even feel as though we are being knocked out of the batters box, but that is when we need to dig our heals in and slug one out of the park.

Well, I had come to that situation after a lot of success in the home building industry. I happened to be raised on construction sites. Not sure how my dad did it, but he had me working with him at an early age. I am serious when I say an early age. I remember being just old enough to have him help me crawl into the pickup truck and I would follow him around. Even employees at the lumber yards and other suppliers would know me and offer me candy or a drink and ask me what I want to be when I grow up. At the age of 4 or 5 I obviously wanted to be a General Contractor just like my dad.

As I look back, I believe that this is where I might have started being a dreamer. I enjoyed helping my dad start with a field full of weeds, trees, and other vegetation and within a few months, there sat a beautiful home that we had built. This was in the Midwest so it was hot and humid in the summer or cold and wet in the winter. We built a lot of our homes on the shores of Lake Erie. This is where my dad taught me the meaning of hard work and not to ever stop until the job was finished. We would even get into trouble with my mom because of getting home too late for dinner, but we had a job to do and we went home when our task for the day was finished, not before.

How many employees will leave at the very minute they are supposed to "clock out?" Actually most will begin to pick up and have everything in place to leave the minute their time is up. You might be saying that is what they should do. After all, they only get paid a certain number of hours and most companies are not paying overtime with the current economy. That is my point.

Anyone who has had a lot of success has committed time and energy doing more than what was expected. You make a living from 8:00 am to 5:00 pm and you get ahead from 5:00 pm to 11:00 pm as I mentioned earlier. Not many people are willing to pay the price of success.

We could get into the definition of success, and in fact, that could be an entire book. I am sure there has been many books written on the topic of the definition of success. I will make a brief statement at this point to define my definition of success so you can feel and know where I am coming from. My definition of success is this. Doing What You Want To Do, When You Want To Do It. This will never happen unless you truly have a desire to accomplish whatever it is for you. This is what I call the "Burning Desire." Just like I have mentioned earlier, most highly successful people have had to pay a price.

If you are reading this book I will assume you are not average and are interested in becoming more successful than making an hourly wage from a J.O.B. It is likely you are interested in building success for you, not for an employer. I have never met anyone who became financially secure working for someone else and only doing their minimum job description. Even in the business world, what do they do when they find someone who is willing to work harder than their piers? They give them a title and put them on salary. What a salary does is allow the business owner to make you work more without a concern of paying you overtime. Every company or employer I have met requires or expect their salary people to work beyond a 40 hour work week.

Why help make someone else to become successful when there are several ways you can work to build your own success? If you are willing to work for it.

This willingness to do whatever it takes reach your dreams, your goals and become a difference maker is critical to building your Burning Desire. If you see no way for you to work and get ahead, or work hard and longer to make more money to save for extra time with your family, or work harder for tangible items, such as a boat, or other fun purchases, or serve the greater good, then of course you will fall into the rut of doing your work and going home.

I have talked to many who have had great dreams and have even set goals while in college. They graduate college and then begin to work. After years in college and paying a lot of money to attend, they get their first paycheck. That is when reality sets in and they realize that they can hardly pay their rent or mortgage and other living expenses with what their education has allowed them to earn.

I can offer several examples, but I will just give you two at different ends of the spectrum. Teachers will attend college for at least 4 years. Then they will need to do some classroom work with another teacher before they can actually apply for a job. If they find a school district that has an opening to hire them, they will make an income of approximately $25,000 to $35,000 per year depending on where they live. This is after spending 4 years of their life learning how to teach and paying an average state tuition of approximately $20,000 per year. They have a total of $80,000 invested along with the four years of their life so that they can earn enough money to live at home with their parents. They might be able to find a place of their own if they have 2 or 3 roommates.

Another career choice might be an attorney. You could take more time in school, usually 6 to 8 years, spend more than $250,000, most of the time much more, so that you can approximately make $45,000 to $50,000 per year for the first several years until you build your experience. All of this is exciting if you love what you do and your goal and ambition is to become the best litigator or the best educator you know and you want to make a difference in that chosen field. We need people for all of the careers. In fact, if that is your goal, hopefully this book will help you develop the Burning Desire to stay in school or go back to school so that you can have your dream become reality. I believe you will need to remain focused and work harder than you ever have if you want to get into the Law School that will put you into a position to build your successful career. Then, while you are working hard after you graduate from school, you will make a much lower income while you pay the price to build your experience and knowledge of the real world of Law.

This is going to be true in any profession you pick. If you have a desire to become successful in any career, the information in this book will help you reach the highest levels of your career and will help you become the best you can be. You will become all that God meant for you to be. With all of that being said, the reason I described the above example is because the majority of the people that attend the colleges do not stick it out and finish. Even for the ones that do finish and get a job, they are so discouraged by their income potential that they fall into the hamster wheel rut of going to work and knowing they will never be able to be the success they once wanted when they started college.

Most college graduates do not work in the field of their degree. Many that quit college do so because they get tired of studying so hard and working in school and not making money. They start working for a lower income thinking they will work hard and make more later. The challenge is the income raises are very far away and never as much as we thought. This is why many have an extremely difficult time having any further dreams.

Many of you that are reading this have fallen into this situation. Yes, there is hope, but you will need to do a major shift in your thinking. You will need to think outside the box. I say you should throw the box away.

In the corporate world they call this a paradigm shift. If I could put this information in bold letters and capitalize every single letter of this, you might be able to understand the importance of these words and thoughts. I can give you all of the information you need to be more successful than you have ever dreamt and reach levels of income that you never thought possible, but if you do not believe you can accomplish these levels, then it will not happen. In order to take action on turning your dreams into goals and having your goals become reality, you not only need to develop your Burning Desire, but you will need to believe you can actually reach your dreams. Without that belief, you will just waist your time "trying" to develop your Burning Desire.

I know I could have been the best home builder and designer in the United States if I would have remained in that career, but my focus changed for several reasons. Much of it had to do with no matter how hard I worked at doing the same thing and no matter how much I wanted to be more successful, doing my current career in the same manner of which I was doing it would not give me the success I wanted.

I have talked to many people who keep thinking they have invested money and time into a business or invested their time into their job and if they just work a little harder or a little longer, they will make more or build what they want. "If you find yourself digging a hole, stop digging." These are the words of the best mentor I have ever had. Although I am sure he heard it from one of his mentors. But yet many business owners keep working on their same businesses digging a deeper hole until they file Chapter 7 BK or they finally give up their business and go to work for someone else.

Remember the concept of leverage and also remember that you need the right tool to reach success. "Doing What You Want To Do, When You Want To Do It." Not many people who work for someone else or do not have a tool to duplicate their efforts will ever be able to reach that principle.

So, at the age of 32 I changed my career. Not just changed my career but went from doing back breaking hard physical work wearing jeans and a t-shirt to wearing a suit and learning all about helping people with their financial picture. I also moved 3,000 miles across the country to begin my new career. I knew no one, I was in a totally different environment because I moved from a small town in the Midwestern part of the United States to the thriving, fast paced, and booming area on the West Coast of the United States. Everything was different. Even the way people perceived finance was completely different.

Most people make comments that I was setting myself up for failure. My own mother told me not to sell my home in the Midwest because it was a beautiful home that I designed and built by myself. I told her I had to sell my home so my family and I would have a place to live in the West Coast. She asked me what I would do if I failed? I informed her that failure was not an option.

I had studied my new career. I talked to people who were successful and people who were not successful in my new financial planning career and I knew exactly what I needed to do. I knew how many people I would have to call to schedule appointments and I knew how many appointments I would need each week to make my goals. I went to making under $25,000 per year to making my goal of $100,000 in my first year. This was in the early 1980's when a $100,000 per year income was in the top 5% in the US. I did this because I had a Burning Desire to make my new career a success. I did this due to having great training by mentors and others who had success. I became the most successful first year representative the company had ever had because I did what I was taught, but I did more than anyone else had ever done. The number of people I was told to meet each week was 10 to 15. I saw a minimum of 15 with my average being 20 to 25 people per week. I tell you this not to impress you, but to impress upon you the benefit of doing whatever it takes to reaching a goal. Why did I do so much? I had a "Burning Desire" to be the best that I could be. I would not settle for anything less.

Due to my success and hard work, I was asked to begin training new people after only four months in my new career. I put myself in the position to earn more income my duplicating my efforts through helping others. Following my Burning Desire helped me make a difference in other peoples' lives, not just for my clients, but for my fellow co-workers.

I studied and asked a lot of questions of people who I thought had success. I evaluated their lifestyle, their income, and their values. One common factor they all had was the way they were able to leverage their time. Either through people or some other method. Even in my profession at the time, I talked to everyone I could and the people who had the most success were the managers and vice presidents who received an override on many other financial planners. Yes, it was possible for an individual to make more than his manager or vice president, but it was unlikely and the individual had to work twice as hard to make the same. So I decided to leverage my time and when asked, I took the opportunity to leverage my time by training others to do what I became good at doing.

I will never forget the first time I realized not everyone had my similar burning desire. This was my first lesson, which helped me understand I needed work on being a good manager. Just because you can sell does not mean you can manage other sales people without learning more about people and becoming a good leader of people.

I was helping a new person set their goals and determine the amount of effort they would have to put into their business to help them become successful. I told her how many people she would need to call and then how many appointments she would need to make. Her comment was one that I have always remembered. She said she did not want to work that hard. I answered her by saying if you want to make $100,000 per year, she would need to do that much activity. She answered me by saying that she did not wish to make $100,000 per year. Her goal was not my goal. Her goal was for her and I needed to help her reach her goal, not mine. This was in the mid 1980's and her husband had a good job and she wanted to build a career for herself but was not interested in putting the same amount of time into her business as what I had done. In other words, she did not have a Burning Desire to make a $100,000 per year. I did, but she did not.

This was my first learning experience in helping people set their goals first and then I would help them accomplish "their" goals and helping them turn their goal into a Burning Desire. This woman ended up building a very nice career in financial planning making a nice income for her family. She was able to develop a Burning Desire but it was not to reach a certain income. Her Burning Desire became something completely different. She wanted to be extremely knowledgeable about a specific area of financial planning. Her dedication to this specific segment required her to study and research much more than anyone else. She used her time to become educated in her specialty and people came to her for information and many of her clients referred her to people that would benefit from her knowledge. Due to her expertise in her area, she did not have to spend as much time making phone calls and setting up appointments. Her referrals happened much quicker than others in financial planning because of her Burning Desire to have the knowledge.

After helping a few people become successful I was asked to become a manager and not just a trainer of people. This happened only 8 months after beginning my new career. At this point I also had responsibility of my personal clients and learning more about the financial field, but now I had to read how to manage people and motivate them to succeed. This would only happen if I committed and spent a lot of time living my Burning Desire.

A long time ago, I learned that there are even some people who cannot create a desire for anything. The hourly working mentality will offer some security because you will know exactly what you will earn for every hour you work. You put in a week's worth of work and at the end of the week or every two weeks, whatever your pay schedule is, you will get paid at the end of the pay period. Some people are totally satisfied continuing to do what they have always done and having what they already have. If you are one of those people, you may want to put this book down now or, better yet, gift this book to a friend who craves more from life beyond what they already have.

You see, the difference is that if you truly want more, you have to do more. More does not mean you work more hours. More does not mean you go to school and learn more so you can earn more. More means that you need to think outside the box a little and not be afraid to work hard at working smart.

When you have the security of knowing exactly what you "will" make at the end of the pay period, you also have the knowledge of knowing exactly what you "will not" make. You will not earn more unless you have overtime but many companies are not offering overtime in this economy. I find it interesting when someone who has an hourly wage type of career and will actually say they don't like to work overtime because if they do it will all go toward taxes. Now this is one way to justify being lazy. I have never heard of a 100% tax. It is true the amount of tax you pay will increase and maybe even the percentage will increase, but you will still end up with more in your pocket at the end of the pay period. Remember this, if you are currently in an hourly pay position. Use that overtime money to save up and do more. The overtime you have now could be just what you need later to begin something big.

For many of us, when we think of having more, we feel a sense of guilt and a suspicion that success is somehow dangerous or that we are not worthy of success financial or otherwise. This is why one must regard success as a "lifestyle" rather than simply turning a profit. Frankly, I struggle to understand how it can be that any given individual would not desire to become the best they can be.

I believe God made all of us in His image and likeness. This does not mean our physical appearance is the same as God's, but that we have a massive ability to learn and to be creative. Does it not follow, then, that we are each special and therefore should have our own special accomplishments? This is why I am going to help you transform your dreams into tangible goals and explain the matter of making goals become reality. Bear in mind, however, that success in this endeavor demands nothing less than being in possession of a legitimate Burning Desire and becoming a Difference Maker.

I also believe God gave us a free will. This free will allows us to be happy with whatever comes our way or it will give us the free will to be determined to be the best that God meant for us to be. When I was in the process of growing personally I did a lot of reading and listening to many people. I forgot who wrote this comment, but I have shared with my lovely wife what I hope people will say about me when I am gone. "The people were better because he came."

I believe it is my purpose in life to help others be better than they ever thought they could be. I want to "make a difference." I truly believe that if you are reading this book, YOU want to make a difference also. It is only a decision away. When we are not motivated that is when self discipline has to kick in. What do you want people to say about you when you are gone?

*Do you have something you want so bad that it hurts?

*Do you have the self-discipline to maintain the direction to reach your Burning Desire?

*How will your Burning Desire help others?

What It Takes to Be a Difference Maker

Do you have the four C's?

It takes a special person to build the type of success that offers financial freedom. To build success that will allow you to "do what you want to do, when you want to do it."

If you can determine your goals and develop your Burning Desire, you will be in the driver's seat to reach a level of success few people will ever know. Once you take these steps and turn them into a habit, you are on your way to building your Burning Desire.

You might have heard the saying, "Success is a journey, not a destination." And it's true. Keep in mind that during this journey your personal development is critical. Listening to well-known speakers, reading their books, and contemplating their ideas will help build the foundation of success: the four C's: Character, Courage, Commitment, and Capacity.

I learned about the four C's from my best and favorite mentor. He predicted that everyone who possesses these traits will be able to build success. So as I create my future, I look for people who either have the four C's already or are willing to work hard to attain whatever C they're missing. In doing so, I built a business with motivated, ambitious people who are already on track for success.

Let's take a look at the four C's and how we can cultivate them.

Character

Most people would like to believe they have character. It's my belief that if you want to know someone's true character, you should give them a challenge and see how they deal with it. After all, it's not the problem that makes us fail or succeed. It's our actions that determine the outcome. A good way of saying this to someone is to just simply say, "You find out what people are made of when you nudge them."

Sometimes our character is built through failure. In fact, most successful people have experienced failures on their way to the top.

One famous example is Colonel Sanders of Kentucky Fried Chicken fame. At the age of 65 he went bankrupt and was driving around the country in a dilapidated car. But after developing his personal chicken recipe, he launched one of the first fast food restaurants that sold more than just hamburgers. The rest, as they say, is history.

Another way we build character is through focused attention. Just as regular exercise leads to physical fitness, daily attention to our character builds moral fitness. I cultivate my strong character by reading and reviewing my goals and priorities every day.

Personally I am the man I am today because of the challenges I've faced and my reactions to those challenges. Some of these challenges were no fault of mine and some were the result of my actions. Some involved personal attacks. Now, being accused of something you haven't done is a difficult challenge to cope with. This is where your personal character has to step up. But if you know in your heart you are on an ethical path, you no longer fear naysayers and critics. Instead you retain your peace of mind while you continue to pursue the right path.

Another word for character might be integrity. The word is derived from the word "integer" which means a whole number. I like to think of it as "a whole person" is one who has Integrity. As a whole person, you make decisions based on the facts available to you – not on seeking an advantage or avoiding discomfort, but on choosing the right and ethical path.

You'll find that it's actually easier to make decisions this way. Once you are asked a question or put into a situation, you act from your strong character and simply respond with the "right" choice. Maybe this sounds outdated in today's world - but if we each work on doing what is right, maybe, just maybe, we can collectively "make a difference."

Courage

Courage is required whenever we need to do something that's unpopular in the eyes of others. I am always amazed at how many people will listen to their family, friends, neighbors, and others who are broke themselves but want to give you advice on building a successful future. They want to give you their opinion; you feel obligated to listen to them. This is what I call *stinking thinking*. Why would you listen to anyone who is not where you want to be? Try looking at it from other perspectives. Would you have a physical trainer who was 50 to 100 pounds overweight? Would you listen to anyone who was failing in the area they are teaching? Probably not.

Yet when people want advice about trying something different, they usually seek out their family, broke friends, or anyone offering an opinion. Courage is when you share your dream with people who tell you it won't work or mock you for thinking it will – and you persist anyhow. You continue pursuing your strategy because you know others who have made it work, so you know that you can do it too if you follow the process taught.

Courage is also required when the effort to reach your goals becomes uncomfortable. Athletes have to practice, work out, eat right, and push themselves to become the best they can be. If they want to be competitive, they have to go beyond the limits of what others are willing to do. Yes, this takes discipline. But it also takes courage to work hard even when others are saying, *It's too hard. It's not worth taking the time from your family. It's not worth giving up this season for the rest of your life.*

I encourage you to have the courage to make a difference in your life and the lives of everyone you'll help.

Commitment

If you want to accomplish any worthwhile task, you must be committed. Surprisingly, some people believe commitment is one of the easier traits to possess. After all, anyone can say, "I'm committed." But stating a commitment doesn't mean it exists. Remember the saying that "what you do speaks so loud that I can't hear what you say." You must learn what tasks and activities need to be perfected to meet your goals. This is why it's important to review your decision carefully to make sure you are willing to commit to it.

I like the saying that when motivation fails, self-discipline steps in. Well, that is what commitment is all about.

Commitment is one of the most difficult traits to have and can be especially tough to maintain. Commitment is comparable to setting goals. People think they have a goal when it is really a wish list. They aren't willing to keep pursuing their goal once any difficulty or negativity arises. Do you know the average person can't take more than 10 rejections? How many times would you ask someone for a date before you stopped asking? Well, if you really wanted the date, you would keep asking. It's the same principle with your goal. Keep striving for it no matter how long it takes. As long as you have a plan in place, you will accomplish the task and reach your goal.

The reason why people stop trying is simple: their goal hasn't become a Burning Desire. But commitment to your goal will help fuel that Burning Desire. Once you commit to reaching a goal that will truly make a difference, then you need to "live" it as if there is no way you can live without it. That is what I explained in the first chapter when describing what a Burning Desire is all about.

Capacity

This is a word most of you probably haven't heard in the context of achieving or even setting goals. Yet this is one of the most important traits to search for when recruiting people to help you build a business. As I have already discussed, many people say they want success and dream about accomplishments. *Capacity* is the ability that already exists in someone when we meet them.

There could be many reasons why an individual would have a capacity to do something. It could be previous training and skill sets that they have already perfected due to experience. Or they could be a "natural" at a certain task. There could even be some physical characteristics which could offer someone a specific aptitude.

But in this context, let's focus on the personal capacity to get things done. For example, being able to communicate with people. Being able to walk into a room and have people listen to you just because of your energy or looks or the way you handle yourself. Yes, some people naturally possess these traits. You could also have skill sets that give you an advantage.

But you must also have the capacity to become adept at your endeavor – to understand what you are studying. For instance, I don't believe I would have the capacity to be a stock analyst. I can be detailed when I need to be, but after a certain point, I just fog over and stop caring. I'm sure some of you can relate to that.

So, how does capacity relate to you reaching your dreams and accomplishing your Burning Desire? You need to be certain of what it will take to reach your goal. If you don't already possess the necessary capacity for the task, yet you believe you really do have the burn to accomplish it, you will need to develop the capacity.

In my experience, this is the only one of the 4 C's that can be developed with hard work. It is not easy to build capacity but you can if the desire is intense enough. Remember, "whatever the mind can conceive and believe, it can achieve."

*Well, do you have the four C's?

*Which one, or ones, do you need to work on?

*Which one is your greatest gift already?

Achieving Personal Success

Personal Traits of High Performers

I was told the story about a young man who had the pleasant opportunity of having dinner with Earl Nightingale, the famous radio personality and producer of self-improvement cassette programs.

Mr. Nightingale made his life's work looking into and reading about successful people and how they built their successes. This young man had long looked up to Mr. Nightingale for his ideas and philosophy.

During the dinner, this young man asked Mr. Nightingale what advice he would give his son if he had one. Based on his knowledge and vast experience, what would be the one thing that would help his son ensure success both in business as well as in his personal life.

Earl told him, "You know, I have often thought about that very question. And after all the years and a lot of thinking, I've come to the conclusion that your success in life, or in business for that matter, can be boiled down to one thing. That is, your rewards will always be in direct proportion to the amount of service you render."

"You only have to look around," he said. "The people who serve others, prosper. The people who don't serve others, don't prosper.

And you can tell just how successful a person is by the amount of service they render to others."

"The problem," he continued, "is that unsuccessful people either haven't learned that great secret, or they don't apply it."

I have always felt Successful people are the ones who develop the habits of doing the things that unsuccessful people are not willing to do. If you remember, I mentioned this a couple of chapters earlier. I will say it again, Successful people make a habit of doing what unsuccessful people do not do.

If you think about what you have tried to do and task that you have tried to accomplish, is this true of the task that became successful? The more you serve your clients, or people in general, and help them satisfy their needs, the more you will prosper.

And as a business owner, business manager, professional person or entrepreneur, serving your customer's needs effectively means that you must do the things that unsuccessful business owners, managers, professionals, and entrepreneurs don't do. The things that those unsuccessful people don't do are the things that most of us don't like to do either.

There is no doubt that it is difficult to work long hours or on weekends when your family is waiting for you at home, and only have a couple of "shoppers" stop by or be stood up for an appointment someone made with you.

It's tough to make telephone calls, only to be met with hostile and rude people on the other end who curse at you or slam the phone down.

It's discouraging to set goals, schedule interviews, explain the technical aspects and benefits of the products and services you provide, overcome customer's objections and misconceptions, and go out of your way to give exceptional service, only to have your customer go elsewhere because they found the same product or service for a few dollars less. Or, maybe you work with a client explaining the perfect strategy for them to help them meet their specific objectives only for them to say, "No".

Enough of these experiences can be discouraging for anyone. And after a while, some people just quit trying. Remember I mentioned that most people can not take more than 10 no's. After they fail, they find it easier to adjust their standard of living downward to match their income, than to adjust their income upward to create their desired standard of living.

They are no longer in control. Inflation dictates the price of things they buy, and competition and luck determine how much they have to spend. Fortunately for them, many of their competitors are in the same situation.

Outstanding success is unusual and hard to come by, and is dependent on many different factors. For some people, it just happens. They're in the right place at the right time, they do nothing special, everything just falls into place for them. Others put in long hours and much work, only to find average success. What is important is that you have the drive and determination to do whatever it takes to build your success. To turn your dream into a Burning Desire.

But a clear understanding of success characteristics, a well executed plan, and certain personal traits can help move you towards your goals more quickly. This is how you develop a Burning Desire.

Here are some personal qualities to consider:

Eight Personal Characteristics For Success

1. Know What You Want

I know I have already discussed setting goals but let's go into this more in depth due to the importance of setting the right goal for you so the true Burning Desire will build for you to put a spark in your life.

Know yourself. Know exactly what you want. So many people enter into a task and spend months and even years in their environment without having any idea of what they want, or what is possible to get out of their life.

In fact, most people are working so hard just living life they don't have time to work on themselves as a person. As a result, they've become complacent with life. This is the worst place to be. They're working to pay the bills rather than building an exciting life which will give them the satisfaction of helping others which will have them Make a Difference.

Take time to analyze where you have come from, where you are now, and where you are going in your job or your career. Then begin to set some meaningful goals. The type of goals that excite you and give you the reason to wake up every morning and get out of bed just as soon as you wake up. You see, if you don't know where you want to go, you will never get any place that will make a difference in your life and then definitely not in anyone else's life. Making the decision to stretch yourself and put in the hard work that will accomplish a successful task is a huge step to creating and building your Burning Desire.

Meaningful goals are the most important requirement for success. When you turn your dream into goals, you have a target to aim for, a purpose for being around, and a direction to travel. Without goals, it's easy to wander aimlessly, getting sidetracked with any thing that comes along.

When you set your goals, think of, "SMART." You should have SMART goals.

Your goal should be *Specific.*

It is important for your goals to be **Specific,** so you will know exactly what you are working towards. Your goal should be clearly laid out so you can think about it and talk about it…even if you just talk about it in your own mind. This will aid in creating the Burning Desire. Identify your goals and the steps to get there so you know what you are trying to accomplish, and know when you accomplish it.

Just to say you want to sell more, or reduce the number of people you talk with to close a sale is not enough. You need to clearly specify your task to reach your goal. Is it 10 more sales per month? An extra $120,000 in monthly sales? Is it helping others at your church through a program that you design and implement within the next 4 months?

Do you think when Roger Bannister broke the 4 minute barrier in running he just decided to do it one day? No, he worked on each step and how it was made. He reviewed his form and made a goal to do each of the changes needed to have his goal become reality.

Whatever your goal, there should be no doubt about what you wish to accomplish and no question to what you are willing to do to accomplish your goal. Remember, as long as it is legal and moral, you can use it and you can do it.

Your goal should be *Measurable.*

That is, there should be a system, or method of determining how you are going to accomplish your goals and what efforts you need to do to attain your goal. By clearly defining your goals as discussed in the previous step, you will be more able to monitor and follow your progress of them. It's important for you to be able to see where you are now and watch your progression towards your goal.

Your goal should be *Attainable.*

If your goal is too high… if there is no hope for you to accomplish it, it will not take long for you to become discouraged, and you will either lose drive and concentration to pursue your goal, or you will abandon your journey. This is the biggest mistake you can make. So, be sure you set the goal right the first time as to not continue when it gets tough.

You should set some smaller goals on the journey to the major goal. This will allow you to have small successes and keep you moving in the right direction. Think of something you can reach with just a little extra effort. The key is "extra" though. You need to always remember to stretch yourself.

Your Goal needs to be *Realistic*

In life, you need to make sure your goals are not only attainable, but are also…**Realistic.** I actually hate that word. I wish I could remove it from the dictionary along with the word, can't. But… it is important to make sure your goal is something that is within your grasp with some hard work and some imagination from you. I talked about this earlier and it is critical to your success.

Your goal should build an image, something that enhances your self-confidence in a positive way. Then, the next time, set a little higher goal. Not much higher, just a little higher. Again, one that you know you can achieve. And that adds on to, and builds your confidence that much more.

Your goal needs to be *Time Sensitive.*

That is, you should set a time limit. This helps you keep on target, not be distracted, and encourages you to complete something you have started. Not only will this help to realize success, but you will build on your self image by accomplishing your goal.

Take your goal and break it down in steps. Be precise and put a time table on each step. Monitor what goes on and what you are doing each day to reach your goal. Just being busy is not helpful but being productive with your time is. So, make sure you know what are your productive activities.

A large goal becomes much more manageable in small pieces. The key is to break your goals into bite size pieces, and place a time deadline on them, for their accomplishment.

2. The Ability To Focus

Many people hesitate to go set a goal or start something new because they think they lack the talents and abilities necessary to succeed. They look at others. They see people who are successful and think that they should have the same talents or skills. Once you work with them and get to know them you will learn they are the same as you or maybe even not as skillful as you are.

The difference is, successful people have developed the ability to focus. A person of average intelligence, who is focused on a clearly identified goal, will consistently outperform the sharpest and smartest people who are not focused.

3. Determine The Price You'll Pay

Earlier this came up in the much simpler version of what it takes to set a goal. Remember I mentioned that you need to think about three things – do you want it, do you need it, can you afford it?

You must determine the price you have to pay to be reach your goal. For everything in life, there is a price. And it must be paid up front. In most cases, it takes sacrifice. Remember some of the stories I shared earlier.

A few years ago, in an effort to get a little exercise and help relieve stress, I bought myself a bicycle. I had fun for awhile, but then a group of experienced riders flew by me one day on their fast, shiny, obviously high priced racing bikes.

Always a competitive person, I decided that I would try to catch them and ride with them. But, try as I might, it was not going to happen. Nothing I did would allow me to catch up to them. That ate on me for about a week, and it was not long after that I found myself back in the bike shop getting the specifications and prices of one of those "fast, shiny, obviously high priced" bikes.

$2,500 later, I was back on the road just waiting for those riders to catch me so I could ride with them. I was completely decked out in cycling shorts and jersey, special shoes, helmet and my new 16speed racer. It was really a sight.

Then, one day it happened. The group of riders came up on me from behind, and I was determined to keep up with them. But a quarter of a mile later, try as I might, I was "off the back." The riders were gone, never to be seen. That really irritated me, again.

So I bought several books, obtained some video tapes, and sought out the help of a neighbor who was a pretty good rider. I worked hard trying to develop my cycling abilities. I rode every morning from 4:30 to 7:30, while my family was still asleep.

I encountered motorists who didn't like cyclists. Some even went so far as to run me off the road and throw bottles at me.

I rode in the rain and cold weather. Well, it was in Southern CA so it was not too cold. I worked hard and eventually hired a cycling coach to help me develop my skills.

Then I entered a local race, and to my surprise I won! This encouraged me so I entered another race. Then another. And another. And I kept winning.

With the new skills and confidence I was developing, I entered the state and national championships, placing very high in both. The riders who used to pass me were now coming to me for help and advice. They wondered how I could consistently beat them when I had not been riding for nearly as long as they had.

What they did not understand was that it was not how long I had been training, as much as what I had put into my training. It was not what I did during the race that counted as much as it was what I did during the long, lonely, solitary hours of training. It was the sacrifices I made that made the difference between being a social rider or the rider who would win races.

The same concept of sacrifice applies to accomplishing any important goal or being the best at what you do in your career. If you want to reap the great and plentiful rewards your goals can provide you, you are going to have to do some not-so-glamorous things at some not-so-convenient times.

You're going to have to do what I mentioned earlier. Make a habit of doing things that unsuccessful people are not willing to do.

That may mean, doing things that will stretch you and make you uncomfortable. It is so very important to know you we're put on this earth to make a difference no matter how difficult it might be.

If you have a family, this may prove to be a hardship on you, but if you are just starting to build your goal, or want to increase what you are currently doing or achieve some new goals, you may have to make that sacrifice.

If you are not willing to make the sacrifices, then you cannot expect to be as successful as someone who is willing to make those sacrifices. Those that are willing live their Burning Desire are the people who will Make the Difference.

4. Self Responsibility

You are totally responsible for the success of your life. There may be setbacks or financial challenges, economic downturns, or problems that affect your level of success. Especially when everything is going well. Life is going well. You are happy and everything just seems to be going in the right direction for your goal to become reality, and then life will throw you a curve ball.

While those things definitely have an impact on you, the way you proceed towards your goal when the going gets tough is what will define you for the long term. It is important to realize that those things are beyond your control, and it's up to you, and you alone, to accept responsibility for YOUR success.

No matter how bad you might have it, no matter what challenges you might have, I assure you that there are many people who have had difficulties and challenges far greater than any challenges you are ever likely to encounter, and somehow, they manage to pull through. And you can pull through too.

Here's a little credo that can help you. It contains just ten, two letter words:

"If it is to be, it is up to me."

That simple one line sentence says it all. It places the responsibility exactly where it should be... directly on your shoulders.

5. Be Committed

Make a total commitment to success. Once you have made the decision to set your goal, follow through with each and every step. Remember to live and develop your goal into your Burning Desire.

I was told in the early stage of my financial planning career a very important lesson that helped me get promoted quicker than most. One of my mentors told me to put myself in a position to say "no". What he meant was to do such of a great job at my position so there would be offers to move upward. Then I could decide if I wanted to take the position at that time or the position that was offered. Because of my hard work I was able to take a position that opened up much sooner than I thought would happen. Yes, it was a stretch for me, but the people making the decision told me that my past success was so outstanding they felt I was the person for the position.

When you make a decision to make it happen, get into it with both feet. Do not allow anything to hold you back. Even more than getting into your goal, see that your goal gets in you. Make a commitment that you are going to succeed, no matter what.

Don't try to work two different jobs or projects at one time. You can not do either of them justice, and you will likely end up frustrated and broke, and never know whether or not you could have reached your goal.

6. The Extra Mile

The sixth personal quality necessary to achieve outstanding success in life is that you must be willing to go the extra mile. It is the "Under promise, over deliver" concept, and can be summed up in the following statement:

"If you are always willing to do more than what you get paid for, the day will come when you will be paid for more than what you actually do."

I will talk more about this in the next chapter where we will discuss relationships. This is where you truly need to go the extra mile. Because when you go the extra mile for people, you will set the stage for that law to take effect. But it is only on that "extra mile" that this works. When you give what might be considered "normal" service, or "adequate" service or – even "good" service, you haven't earned the right to expect that law to work for you.

In fact, even performing "knock-out" service often is not enough to gain you the advantage. We have all come to expect that from everyone.

You have really got to do something special in order to gain an advantage in today's highly competitive marketplace. Remember *"There's no traffic jam on the extra mile."*

7. Control Your Time

The seventh quality is that you must master and take control of your time. Time is an expendable commodity. Each one of us has the same 24 hours in each day. When those hours are gone, they cannot be replaced. They are gone forever, never to be recaptured.

You must treat your time as precious, and guard it wisely. Do not let anyone disrupt you or take you away from the focus you have on your goals. People who do not have goals are used by people who do. If you let others draw you away from your goals, you are simply saying that their goals are more important than your goal.

If you are serious about reaching your goal and Making a Difference – really serious, then this is one of the most important areas to defend. Control your time!

8. Persistence And Determination

Number eight, is to develop persistence and determination. From time to time you will encounter setbacks or reach levels where it seems like nothing is going right. There could be many different challenges that pop up all at once and you can't help but wonder why is this happening?

You seem to be spending more time in a defensive posture than you do in moving forward to reach your goal. Now is not the time to give up. Now is the time to dig in and begin to determine that you are going to Make a Difference. I always told my children when they were young kids, winners never quit and quitters never win. Obviously I heard that from someone but I do not remember from whom.

You have to be determined not to fail and go backwards after you worked so hard to get where you are. Your strategy should be to keep moving forward and keep doing what helped you get to where you are. Remember how it felt and what you did to get where you were before the challenges came. Eventually things will change.

If you have done any reading or listening to people who have been successful, it is always the challenge that made them stronger. I truly believe that you can do anything with God's help. We all have so much more strength than we realize. Use what He gave you and then you will Make a Difference.

*Do you offer a service, which will truly help people? If so, what is it, or better yet, what are they?

*Re-read all 8 personal characteristics and then write down how you stack up to each and every one of them. The time you spend on this task will completely change the direction of your success. Are you willing to take the time and effort?

Finding Your Burning Desire to Make a Difference

I would like to get right into helping you have your dreams become your goals and then working to have your Burning Desire become reality.

All of the success you desire is possible. We have talked about developing the Burning Desire and some examples of what it has taken for others. There is much more that could be discussed, but let's move onto making it happen.

You have to know that the Burning Desire is possible and this is what you should learn during your research. You need to learn what others have done within the same field. Learn what people have done that works and what they have done that has not worked. I had a mentor that told me how every example is a good one. It might even be an example of how "not" to do something.

I would suggest spending most of your time with people that have been successful. Not just successful but the top of the class type of success. Ask questions and learn their daily activity. Learn how they think and how they talk. Find out what they have read and what they have listened to that has helped them build their success. This will take time, but will save you so much time during your growth period.

I remember when recruiting someone in my financial career, he wanted to be as successful as I was so he made a comment how he would wear what I wore, talked like I talked, worked more hours than I did, and even wore the same shoes as I did to make sure he would be successful. This sounded great and as his mentor and trainer, I was excited that I found someone willing to pay the price. Then after 6 months of doing half of what I was doing, he could not keep up the pace. I do not say this to impress you but to impress upon you that the only reason he could not build his success was because he did not have a Burning Desire that would drive him. He had more of a dream than a Burning Desire. His wife had a great job as a Trauma nurse and he had previously worked for a large company that had given him security. Unfortunately he had the hourly mentality even though he wanted more, it was only a wish or a want, but did not turn into a Burning Desire. While writing about this, I wish I would have known then what I know now and I could have helped him develop his burn. Well, I could have tried, but you see, this is what I have recently learned about helping people become successful. You cannot help people do something they do not truly want to do after they consider what it will take to accomplish their goal.

You probably have heard the saying, talk is cheap. Well, a lot of people talk the talk, but they do not walk the walk. We could come up with many different sayings demonstrating this same concept. The reason why there are so many sayings regarding this is simple. It is a major component of success. The decisions we make versus the desires we have.

Scientist tell us that we use a very small percentage of our minds. I believe we do not only use our minds to learn and think, but the creative side of our minds and the driving side of our personalities as well.

You might say that it is your ultimate goal to make a certain amount of money per year. I actually believe that most people are afraid to have a Burning Desire because they do not trust that they deserve that much success, or that should be able to reach that lofty of an income level, or even be able to have an extravagant home or automobile.

Yes, it is totally conceivable to have a Burning Desire that is not legal, moral, or ethical. Well, what could that be? I can hear you now - "I thought that any goal we are willing to work for should be a great goal."

Remember what we have heard repeated over and over; "No pain, no gain." If I am willing to work hard for anything, it should be worth all the blood, sweat and tears once I accomplish it. Many of us were taught this crucial lesson during our athletic careers when we were younger. Now, some would call that child abuse! It is surprising how we survived the punishment of our youth.

But, yes, some people have a Burning Desire to take inappropriate actions toward someone else. It could be to "get even" or to just plain hurt someone else or somehow take advantage of someone else or "to get ahead." Take that which is not ours. Have enough money to control someone or something. There are countless other actions that would not be appropriate but do crop up from time to time. I believe it is a very simple task to learn whether your goal which becomes a Burning Desire is an appropriate one for you and can make a positive difference in the world.

Life is all about how you feel. To say this, I have to assume that you have a solid ethical base upon which to grow. It is possible that I assume too much, but after reading what it takes to develop a true Burning Desire, do you not agree that it is in fact impossible to have one that is not legal, moral, or ethical?

I want to think that, as humans, we have the God gene inside all of us and down inside there someplace, we want to do more good than bad. I know for certain that we begin that way. The environment, what we have seen and heard, and actions taken toward us determine how we ourselves will develop. These are all special circumstances that you will personally have to keep in mind while developing your personal Burning Desire.

Some of you can have a Burning Desire at a drop of a hat. I believe that is why this topic has always been interesting for me. Being able to create a Burning Desire has helped me accomplish task that many people told me were impossible. Doing the unbelievable. Even reaching levels of success sooner or quicker than most people thought possible. This can only happen when you feel the burn. Feel the desire to do whatever it would take to reach the goal you put in front of yourself. Some people reach levels of success in business when no one thought there was a market for what they were doing. Some far exceed expectations of what is even humanly possible. We have all heard the story about breaking the 4 minute mile. Doctors said a human being could not run a mile in less than 4 minutes without his heart bursting. The barrier was broken because Roger Bannister had a Burning Desire to do so. Now at the highest level of competition the barrier is broken each time.

We could go all the way back to Christopher Columbus' days and discuss what drove him to sail to the New World when everyone told him the earth was flat and if he sailed too far he would fall off the edge and never return. Do you think Christopher Columbus just woke up one morning and said, Gee, I think I will sail to find a new world to live in. I don't think so. He had to have a real Burning Desire to accomplish a task that had never been accomplished before. Columbus also had to do detailed research before he left the dock to sail to the New World. While doing his research and learning more about the world, the ocean, the boats that he would travel in, the food he would take, the people he would have with him and many other facts he needed to know so he would succeed, this is what developed his "Burning Desire."

Many broken records in sporting events were accomplished the same way...the athlete had a Burning Desire to be the Best at what they did. They worked hard, envisioned their goal becoming reality over and over again until it was part of them. I am certain you have heard of special people who have had injuries or accidents and have still accomplished high esteemed benchmarks. The people that do these unbelievable accomplishments can only do them with a major Burning Desire.

I once heard a special young woman who lost her arm to a Shark attack say a memorable statement. Her reason for living and her life's ambition meant so much to her because she wanted to be a pro surfer her entire life. Even though she was only in her teenage years, to her, that was a lifetime. Just before she reached her level of professional status, the shark took her arm. Now, I am not a surfer, but I believe it is very difficult to get up on the board, keep your balance and do the top level surfing it would take to be sponsored in the Pro circuit if you only have one arm. But when her dad was helping her get back in the water and surf again, he told her that it would not be easy. Her comment was "I don't need easy, I just need POSSIBLE".

This young lady went on to be a pro surfer and when asked about your tragedy, she said her determination was to help other people know they can do whatever they believe. She is a spoke's person for many children and young adults who have had tragedy strike their life but she gives them hope.

I believe too many people do not develop success in life because they do not think BiG enough. If someone is making $8 an hour and you tell them if they do something different they could make $25,000 per month. How would they ever be able to believe that they could go from making less than $1,000 per month to making $25,000 per month. So they will never even begin to believe and take action to build anything that is unbelievable, to them, at least.

If you have had any personal development training or have done any reading of books that discuss positive attitudes, you might say, anything is possible. Yes, it is, but you first have to believe it is possible.

The way you obtain your belief is to do your homework and know that it is possible. If you live your goal and learn options to make it work, then you can accomplish the impossible. While dreaming, learning, and living your goal, then you will have the opportunity to build and develop your "Burning Desire".

I have talked to so many high achievers that have told me they could not sleep, they could not eat right and sometimes they even had difficulty doing anything else, until they found success in their endeavor. This is called a "Burning Desire".

I know we've all heard about goals. But it's been my experience that most people do not know how to create goals that are obtainable or believable. Now this is an extremely tough subject because I do not want to use the word "realistic" or any other word that suggests limitations. So let's talk about goals and the steps you can take to develop goals you can turn into dreams – and how you can turn those dreams into reality after they become your burning desire.

If you are 5 feet tall and have a goal to become a professional basketball player, or if you weigh 130 pounds and have a goal to become a professional football player, that would not be an achievable goal for most people. In fact, we could even use the term "not realistic" here.

In considering your life's ambitions and your short-term goals, you should first focus on what you enjoy doing. I had an extremely successful friend tell me that while some people think they should "do what they love" to be successful, his thoughts were more in the line that people "do what they must." While I partially agree with him, it will definitely help if you at least like what you are doing. I have also learned that the more you know about something, the more you will like and eventually love that activity.

This is one reason I believe it's critical to do your research on your goals and talk to people who are where you want to be. If you truly despise working with people, then it might be best to consider a career where it's minimal, such as analysis, research or software design. Some people believe they do not like to sell, so then they assume any people-oriented career wouldn't work for them. But once they understand that successful sales are about helping people get what they want through a specific offering, then those careers become reframed as fun and helpful, rather than talking prospects into buying something that they don't want or need.

Now let's talk about how to figure out if your goals are right for you. Notice I said *right*, not *realistic* or *possible*. All things are possible. A favorite saying of mine, "If you have the faith, God has the Power." So let's start with Goal Setting 101. First you should ask yourself these three questions.

"Do I want this?"

"Do I need this?"

"Can I afford this?"

I will break these down because they might not make sense to you on the surface.

Do I want this?

This appears to be self-explanatory, but it really isn't. Many people want things that they don't have. They also covet things that other people have. Honestly answering "Do I want this?" will confirm if you are working towards a personally fulfilling goal. Think about both the short term and long term consequences of your goal. Is it sending you in a direction you can happily see yourself in? It is very important that you genuinely want this result for yourself and aren't pursuing it for someone else.

This is where I part ways with my friend who said *do what you must, not what you love.* The way I see it, your goal might not be your passion now but it could help you live your passion later. Your goal could be part of paying the price to reach your desired destination. Success cannot be paid for but it can be bought on the installment plan every day. So keep all of this in mind when asking the question, "Do I want this?"

Another important factor to consider is whether your goal will help others. Personally I don't believe you will be truly successful in any endeavor unless it's beneficial to others. You might be surprised at how much the desire to help people and make a real difference can affect your level of ambition towards your goal.

The next question is, *Do I need this?* This is more complex. Many goals will be disqualified right here. Yet many laudable goals will also be answered with a NO at first. Let's be honest – most high achievers do not really *need* some of their extravagances. Who actually needs a 10,000 square foot home on the ocean? Why would anyone truly need a Bentley or other expensive cars? Now you see why this question is more complex.

The tangible goal becomes a "need" when you build it to be your Burning Desire. Unless you win the lottery to buy your expensive home or luxury car, it was a Burning Desire before you achieved it. Many of our needs are only needs because we have thought about them often and intensely and lived them out in our minds. I covered a lot of this in Chapter 1 when we defined Burning Desires and then again in Chapter 3 when we discussed how to build your Burning Desire. Remember, this is why most goals are not achieved. They never became a "need" or a "burn."

The last and most important question you have to ask to create a true goal is, *Can I afford this?* This question is the most complex of all. When we think of affording something, we consider money. But in this case, the goal could require time and energy. Can you afford the time? Can you afford the energy? I have previously emphasized the commitment necessary to accomplish a Burning Desire. After all, some accomplishments will take time away from family and friends. Some will involve times where you must sacrifice sleep, do a lot of traveling, eat poorly or forego your regular workout routine.

It's important to consider these factors in advance because achieving a high level of success requires a massive commitment. It will always be inconvenient. Again: you have to give up a season to have a life. Many financially successful people I've interviewed went through a period when their success was a driving factor for them – when their success was, in fact, the most important facet of their life at that specific time. This happens in the corporate world or even as an entrepreneur building a business. Many business owners don't have a family life; their business ends up owning them instead of them owning their business. This is why the third and last question is the most complex but also the most important.

If you are dreaming of a business or special job and you are willing to put in the effort and sacrifice time with friends and family, then commit to it. Do not let your friends and family down. It won't work if you promise to take your children on a vacation to Hawaii by the end of next year, and then fail to earn the success necessary to take them. You've not only let yourself down, but your children as well. You might tell your friends that right now you are devoting your energies to building a position of financial means and will spend more time with them in two or three years. Then five years later you're still working at your goal but not quite giving it 110% and therefore still haven't reached the level of success you needed to spend that time with your friends. Now you've lost credibility with them. They might become negative, saying what you are doing is not working and your efforts aren't worth it. Of course, only you can determine that. Sometimes our goals are going to take longer than we think or are more difficult to accomplish than we initially predicted. Remember, if it was easy, everyone would be financially successful and the lake would be busy on Wednesday, not just on Saturday and Sunday.

*Is your Goal a dream or a Burning Desire?

* Write down and go through the process of, do you need it, do you want it, can you afford it?

*What has been your biggest accomplishment up to this date?

Who is the most successful person you can have lunch with? What questions would you ask this person? Now make an appointment to do it.

Implementing Your Burning Desire

Life is full of challenges. Having a goal and turning it into your Burning Desire requires a total commitment. You need to live your dream before you accomplish it. This does not mean spending money or buying something before you can afford it, but it does mean living out your dream in your mind. You must envision it over and over again. High achievers are rarely surprised or overly excited when they accomplish their goal because they have already lived it on a mental level many, many times.

Remember: whatever the mind can conceive and believe, it can achieve.

Do you believe you can turn your goals into reality?

So now you have what you believe is a real goal. A goal that you want. A goal that you need. A goal you can afford.

Do you believe you can turn this goal into reality? By now you should believe that you can do it if you have been retaining my message in the book so far. But let's examine a few more fundamental aspects of your belief system.

First, you must take action. Most of us believe that we will take action when we are motivated to do so. Unfortunately it doesn't work that way. There are many times when we won't be motivated – and that is when self-discipline needs to kick in. You will need to take action and you will need to know what action to take.

Earlier I mentioned doing research regarding your goal. This research will help you identify those specific steps to take. It will also help you answer the questions we just discussed, especially the question of "Can I afford it?" Remember again the time and energy required to achieve your goal.

I was once told that success comes from self-discipline and organization; over the years I've found this to be more relevant than most people would think. Self-discipline is critical, because there will always be challenges and obstacles to overcome. Also helpful: organizational skills, which can help eliminate or at least minimize confusion and challenges.

If you plan to take action on any goal, you must have a plan. We've all heard the saying that most of us spend more time planning a two week vacation than we do planning the rest of our life. You might think this is funny, but I have personally witnessed this dynamic at many levels while doing financial planning and personal development sessions.

Taking the right action requires having an effective plan in place. The type of activity that you do to reach your goal is critical. There's a difference between staying busy and being productive – and if you aren't being productive, you probably won't reach your goal.

While doing training in the corporate world, I became proficient at a concept known as time management. Personally I prefer to call this "Activity Management." The premise is this: everyone has 24 hours in a day, but it is what we do with the time that makes the difference. Think of the most successful person you know. They have the same time each day as you have. Even if you think of the richest person you've ever heard of, they too only have 24 hours per day. The secret is using those hours strategically and intelligently.

Activity management will become the best tool you have for reaching your Burning Desire. If you have done much reading in the past or if you are over the age of 40, you are probably saying right now, "Oh, I have heard this before." I believe you have not heard it explained in the way I will explain it now.

Your first step is to break down exactly what must be accomplished. The next step is to break that list down into tasks and rate the importance of each task. Every business or endeavor has a desired end result such as getting paid; outline the steps that will accomplish that result in the shortest timeframe.

One trick is identifying the best time of day to accomplish those tasks. During that timeframe, your focus should be on those tasks and those tasks only.

Let's use the example of building a financial planning practice. Part of your business plan is scheduling time to talk to prospective clients about your business. The most important task then would be to schedule the best time to approach these prospective clients. If you wish to contact people after work hours, then evening time will become the highest priority for making those phone calls, with your daytime hours reserved for calling businesses or retired people. Now you have your priorities. No other activity should be allowed during these timeframes. Don't make excuses and spend your "prime time" handling paperwork or filing. Devote those critical hours to your priority tasks.

Another example would be any type of business where transactions happen only during daytime hours. Now making calls and seeing people during the day becomes your priority. If you have a job and are expected to be working at your desk or behind a cash register to collect the sale, that becomes your priority activity. You could have the best customer service of any clothing store when it comes to picking out clothes for someone and helping them with the correct color for their complexion, but if you don't finalize the sale at the register, your business will fail or you will lose your job.

To summarize, you must determine the critical activity necessary for success. This becomes the highest priority. Yes, all of the minor tasks of your business or job have to be accomplished, but identifying those top priority tasks is essential. Prioritize those and use your self-discipline to accomplish them promptly and efficiently.

That brings us to the next important part of activity management: consistency. Here's an analogy from my own life. In 1995, I reached a personal goal by getting my private pilot's license. While flying I learned that I had to give the plane full throttle at takeoff, but after it hit cruising altitude, I could cut back on the power and sometimes fly at less than half of what the initial climb required.

Reaching most of our goals is exactly the same. When you kick off your task, and get into the groove of calling people or selling clothes, you build a momentum that makes it easy to push forward. Even if someone says no, you simply proceed to the next prospect and ask again. You're on a roll. But if you receive a few no's and get discouraged and stop calling, your momentum drops. You decide to take a day or two off so you can get your head on straight. Then one or two days turn into a week or even two. Now you have to takeoff from the runway again and use full power and extra fuel to climb back to a cruising altitude.

So the key word here is consistency. Plan your work and you will plan to succeed. But consistency in executing your plans is just as critical. Another saying I heard many years ago was that *Successful people do things that unsuccessful people are unwilling to do*. Well, I changed that to *Successful people make a habit of doing things that unsuccessful people are unwilling to do*.

Now we come to another key word that's fundamental to success. This word is *tenacity*. Many top performers believe that persistence is the enemy of failure. If you are working a proven strategy, then you will never fail - although of course you can quit. What does this mean? That if you never quit, you will be successful. It becomes only a matter of time. The most common weakness in people who take longer than expected to reach their desired level of success is a lack of consistency. But if you maintain your tenacity, it will lead to consistency – and consistency will lead to success.

Now it's time to talk about why the Activity Management is vital to your success. Previously I mentioned how you make a living from 8:00 am to 5:00 pm but you get ahead from 5:00 pm to 10:00 pm. I believe you need to have this mindset to truly be successful to the point of where you can "do what you want to do, when you want to do it." So let's talk about another result of activity management techniques: maintaining a happy family life during your rise to success.

When I was at the height of my corporate career and being pulled in many directions due to my ambition to be the best Vice-President, I had to learn how to accomplish more than anyone else while still enjoying time with my family. At the time I had two great kids who were very involved in activities that were a little more intensive than typical childhood pursuits. One was riding horses at a competitive level while the other was competing in Regional Junior Golf. My children were the two most important people in my life and I loved spending time with them. Which meant I had to focus on the quality of our time together, not the quantity.

Sometimes while helping people develop their professional potential, I've heard them express the importance of spending time with their children. "I want to be there for them when they come home from school," they say, "or spend time with them in the evening." Yet when I asked for more details, it would sound more like this kind of scenario. Everyone in the family would eat at different times and the parents would watch TV as the six-pack of beer disappeared throughout the evening. If one of the children came in and asked mom or dad a question, they would hear, "Don't bother me now. I'm watching this TV show and it's almost over."

This might sound like an extreme example, but how many times have you seen that kind of scenario play out? I will never forget one Saturday in the beginning of my Vice President timeframe, when my children were 8 and 10 years old. I had been working from early morning until late at night for several weeks. Obviously this was before I learned how to do my personal Activity Management. I was so tired one Saturday afternoon that I started falling asleep in my easy chair. Just then, one of my children asked me to do something with them. I asked if we could do it just a little later after I got some rest. They agreed and went off to play. When I woke up several hours later, the afternoon was over and it was already dinnertime. Disappointed, I apologized to my children. That night is when I decided to concentrate on quality of time as I could not offer them the quantity of time that some other parents might give.

Because of my Activity Management development, within just a couple of years, we were able to enjoy special activities that many parents couldn't do with their children. Due to my commitment to creating financial success, my daughter was able to ride and compete in horse shows and my son was able to golf at the finest country clubs. We spent vacations in Hawaii and enjoyed time together on the ocean. We were also able to move into a nice home inside the country club gates and join the club's golf organization so my son could play every day. Eventually he became a PGA member. Today he owns a thriving golf academy in Southern California, while my daughter became a successful horse trainer. I like to think this is because of the quality of time I devoted to our family.

So many of us don't realize how often our children observe our actions. Your success affects more than just you; as your children witness and copy your behavior, success becomes a family tradition. Keep this in mind as you choose your activities and plan your schedule. Optimizing your weekly schedule will allow you to accomplish your priority activities while scheduling in quality personal time. It takes discipline to do this consistently. But an effective Activity Management strategy is critical to helping you realize your goals. Once again: everyone has the same 24 hours per day.

In summary, I personally believe it is worth making the decision to "go for it" and build success NOW. Find the tool that helps you replicate your time and effort and then work hard to accomplish your success. Most opportunities will allow you to build financial success within 5 to 10 years if you use an appropriate activity management style and focus your effort on high-yield activities. Maintain your tenacity and consistent behavior and never give up.

Winston Churchill was once scheduled to deliver a commencement speech to one of the top colleges in the country when he unfortunately became very ill. He was very old and not in the best of health anyway. Yet he still felt he had something special to offer the college graduates. He slowly walked up the steps, across the stage and said just these words: "Never, never, never give up."

Let's say you are part of a sales force that needs to have the capacity to relate directly to individuals and help them to understand how whatever you are promoting is going to help them achieve their goals. In order for people to "buy" whatever you have in mind to sell, your sustained success relies upon having your clients actually feel as though it is their decision because either a) they need it; or b) they want to have it very badly. We will talk about the relationship part of life later.

I once had an extremely successful financial planner who drove an old, and I mean really old, beat-up Buick. Nothing against

Buicks - my dad always bought the best and highest quality Buick made. An important detail here is that we were doing business in a very affluent market in Southern California. Even though he was a success, in fact the most successful planner among a hundred top-quality people, he just did not feel that it was important to update his wheels and rather felt that it was more wise and prudent for him not to burn his resources on a shiny, new car. At this time in the history of the financial planning field, and also since this particular planner was relatively new to the field and still cobbling together his client base, most of his meetings were held at the client's home. Many planners would do this during their initial growth phase of their business to make it as convenient as possible for the potential client. It kept things very streamlined for the client to have instant access to all of their financial information and it was much easier to embark upon the all-important relationship that is required to do true financial planning and not just "selling an investment".

I asked this top planner if any of his clients had commented on his car and I could not believe what he told me. He said, "Well no, because I usually park about one block away." I sat down with this top producer in his field and reviewed his own finances and we determined that, without any financial stress on his part, he would be able to purchase a two or three year old Mercedes Benz. I suggested that he park in the client's driveway and, without being obvious, have them walk out to the car with him after the meeting. He would deliberately leave something in the car that he wanted to give the potential client after the initial meeting.

Even I, who had suggested the idea, found myself shocked at the response that the nicer car had among his business clients. People have a natural preference for doing business with people who have been successful in their own business dealings. People want to follow leaders rather than losers and, as much as some of you may not want to admit it, many, I mean **many** people make a decision about **YOU** within the first forty-five seconds of meeting you and they will *definitely* make a snap decision about doing business with you or trusting you in any area of their business or even any type of decision that has to be made within the first meeting with you. You have to put your best foot forward and sometimes, that means doing what you must in order to look good, talk well, and polish many other characteristics that we will discuss.

So, the take-away here is that tangible goals absolutely do have their place. Please bear in mind that I am not advocating you go broke just to look good - that is why it is fundamental to have a general goal to succeed so that you can afford all the tools you need to become more successful at what you do. Another statement you just may have heard before: "Success is a journey, not a destination."

You may also have as a goal some kind of specific accomplishment at your work place, or reaching an important benchmark in your own business. I have a friend who owns a cigar business. His Burning Desire to succeed in his business is so intense that he has even told his family not to call him or even bother asking him for a single thing until his business is where he wants it to be. He has been inspired to build the biggest cigar business in his entire state. At one of his shops, he has built the biggest humidor in the entire state and now markets his business with that advantage.

He did not simply open up shop and proclaim that he was going to build the best cigar business in the state. He went about doing his research first. It took him twelve years and roughly seven-hundred visits to cigar shops of all types in a large number of different countries. He studied the industry comprehensively and then got down to business. He opened his first shop and had a plan in mind of exactly what type of setup he would have. He put the plan into place and did whatever was necessary to obtain the desired outcome.

Now, five years into his first shop, he is only one month away from achieving his ultimate vision for the shop. He has opened another location and has a plan in place to open a specific number of operations. He is constantly doing more research on the hows, wheres, and whens.

Why is it that he has been so driven to become the best in his field? I can't speak for him on that, but he most certainly has the requisite "Burning Desire" to succeed at the highest level of competition. He is giving up everything in his life to satisfy his Burning Desire. Some people would say that he does not have his priorities right, and that could be what you suspect in your mind, but this is his goal and he understands that he needs to give up some of his short-term desires for long-term success.

In just a few, short years, he will be able to do whatever he wants to do whenever he wants to do it because of what he is building **now**. Too many people focus on short-term pleasures and then they find themselves giving up on their long-term desires. Success is paid up-front and mediocrity you will pay for the rest of your life. Again, I will repeat that you have to give up a season for the rest of your life.

Take a look at your goal. What do you have to do so your Burning Desire can become reality. I used the cigar shop owner as an extreme example because his goal was that important to him. Working hard now and using delayed gratification is one of the hardest characteristics to build. You will have many obstacles and many people who will be more negative than you could imagine. So do your research and put your plan together so you can begin your journey.

I also have a friend that worked for 5 years in the basement of his home. He set up an office in his basement to manage and run his Land Development business. He bought a parcel of land where he envisioned a fabulous prime development. He dug in and as he did his research and made his development become reality, he was told it would never work. He was even mocked by many people that had been in the business much longer than he had. There were very successful people that said they would buy the land from the Bankruptcy Court after he failed. The local Newspaper even did stories on the "crazy" man who wanted to build a development which included a top rated golf course in an area that would never grow. He purchased a large mountain that was in the middle of the parcel and then donated it to the city so that everyone would benefit from the beauty of having a mountain that did not have homes all over the side of it, but have the mountain remain in its original desert beauty.

After many years this project became one of the most successful esteem communities within the entire western United States. The project also made him tens of millions of dollars and was all worth the hard work, criticism, and hardship he went through to build "his" project. Never give up was his driving force because he had a "Burning Desire" to complete his project.

I could mention many more examples from this same developer. Another successful business person called this man the Donald Trump of Developers. In my eyes, he is, because of the tenacity he maintained but also because of the foresight he had. He started with a plan in mind. He put his efforts into learning everything he could about building the Best. Then he did it. Why, because he created a Burning Desire.

*Do you understand what a Burning Desire is yet?

*What is it that you want so bad, it hurts? And what are the steps you are willing to take to make it happen?

*Do you quit trying once it becomes difficult or gets complicated? Or do you just put your head down and figure away to make it work? Give examples of either or both.

*Do you have the Tenacity to get what you truly want?

Making a Difference

Building Success through Relationships

We have talked a lot about success and how to create it through building your personal characteristics for success. Now we will discuss what you need to complete your success package and make a difference.

You will never be a truly successful individual emotionally until you can perfect the ability to build relationships. This has been saved for the end of your journey to success because it is the most important. Even if you have developed your Burning Desire, you will not be able to live and appreciate your success without building relationships that last.

My view about building a business and building relationships might differ from a few other trainers but all of the successful people who help others feel relationships are important. Remember, they don't care how much you know until they know how much you care.

There are many different types of relationships. Ranging from the moment a father and mother hold their child for the first time and they instantly know they would walk through a brick wall or even give their life for the precious baby in their arms to the distant relationship that all veterans have knowing that they all gave some and some gave all. Many of the vets have never met each other but they would fight for the protection of a fellow veteran. The same goes for first responders. Police are all brothers of blue. Firemen the same. Race car drivers are extremely competitive on the track but if one of them gets into trouble, the true professional driver will be there to help the other one.

Just look around. There are so many ways to be connected to each other. As I write this, our society and country are going through some difficult times. We just went through a presidential election where many people do not care for either candidate. Professional athletes are not standing for the National Anthem to show their dissatisfaction of the state that our country is in. When society needs to come together, just a few are trying to tear it apart. Some are doing it unknowingly while some are purposely wanting to destroy our way of life. Freedom as we know it today.

Let me ask you, what would be the best way to attack a united country? The obvious answer is to divide it. I hope and pray every day that our country will come out at the other end of this devastating time much stronger and better because of it.

My important point is…relationships can build you or destroy you. I want to help you learn how to build the type of relationships that will build you personally and professionally.

To begin this conversation should be simple – use the golden rule. Treat others and you would like to be treated. Honestly, that is the beginning of our challenge. Many people who treat people poorly and have no sense of concern for others were raised that way. Living in a very broken home while growing up, being physically abused as a child or young adult, being pushed to excel by a parent who wants to look good because their child is doing well, or in some cases spoiling a child so much that they do not know what it means to work for anything they have. Thanks to a few psychologist writing books a few years back that were telling parents to change the way their children were being raised. To talk to them and reason with them. Allow them to make decisions and let them learn on their own. To award them for trying to do something regardless how much effort they put into it. All of these suggestions and many more created a generation of young adults that have a feeling of entitlement. They want the success their parents have had but they want it now and don't feel they need to work for it as their parents did. Frankly, most of them do not even realize how hard their parents worked to give them what they had while growing up.

The other interesting fact is that most of these young adults do not have the communication skills needed to build relationships. That is what concerns many of us the most. I realize that technology has come a long way and it is here to stay. There are many benefits of the new technology. But as long as we have our own minds and need to communicate to use the technology it will be important to communicate with other people. And the best way to have someone trust you and rely on you is to build a relationship with them.

Let's get into some actual ways to build a relationship. Many articles about being a good conversationalist have been written. People want to be interesting. People want to be liked. Many of these articles talk about the best way to be a good conversationalist is to listen. Yes, that is true. To listen more than you talk. I always say God gave us two ears and only one mouth. That is so we will listen more than we talk.

I remember when I was transforming from the blue collar industry to the corporate world and the board rooms. I had a mentor at the time that finally took me aside and just looked me in the eye. He said, "Steve, you have a lot to offer. But…you also have a lot to learn and the best way to do that when you are around people is to listen. Stop talking so much." I knew immediately what he was talking about. I didn't realize it while I was doing it, but as soon as he mentioned it and brought it to my attention I could feel inside that he was right.

As I built my success in the corporate world and was at the point of talking to groups of people, sometimes a few thousand, I was always amazed how people would come up afterwards or see me later in the hotel and ask a question. Then without taking a breath, they would begin to tell me how they do things. The very task that they asked me about! By the time they were done telling me what they were doing, it was time to leave and I never did speak to them to answer their specific question.

It didn't bother me at first and then I started realizing it was my responsibility if I really wanted to help them Make a Difference, then I needed to stop them when they started talking after they asked me the question. So I would just put my hand up after they asked the question and ask if they would like me to answer their question. They would always say, of course. Then I was able to offer some individual guidance for them. Even then, that was a time of building a relationship with the person. This type of relationship could be considered an interactive relationship.

I have also learned to appreciate the word, transparent. Many people have a tendency to say, "let me be honest with you". Well, that is insinuating that you have not been honest in the past. Or that if you don't state that fact, that you might not be honest. This is when I decided to use the phase, "let me be transparent with you."

You might ask, when would you use that statement? Let's say that you are giving some guidance to someone and you need to say something to help them, and you know it might be something they do not want to hear. It could be a character flaw that if changing this flaw would help them. It could be anything that might be difficult for the other person to hear. I learned a long time ago, to be a good leader it is important to be transparent.

Some management people are not able to be so transparent and therefore very difficult to build a good and positive type of relationship with their employees or the people that they manage. In today's world if you want to be a good manager you have to be a good leader at the same time. This is all do to the fact that relationships have become much more important than they use to be.

So, if you are going to listen more than you talk, how is this done appropriately or done in a beneficial manner. The first strategy is to ask the appropriate questions. How can you find out what someone is wanting or needing if you don't ask? I also believe even after you know or have an idea of what they want or need, if you just tell them what you think, how will that help the person for the long term? People need to be taught how to think for themselves and how to progress on their own. Yes, sometimes telling can guide them in the right direction, and if they are an exception instead of the norm, they will remember what you told them and use that information later. Most people learn better and the information sinks in more if they talk it through and discover much of the thought process on their own. This is how it will make sense to them. They will discover the answer using their mindset and their behavior style. Then, it will be with them and they can pass it on much easier.

Recently my wife and I had lunch with my youngest son and his girlfriend. I enjoy seeing my son very much and he has moved out of state from where we live so both of us were looking forward to seeing him and hearing how everything is going in their lives. What my wife and I were both concerned about was how do we carry on a long conversation with them. For some reason, they have always been difficult to "build that relationship".

I love him dearly because he is my son. Remember I talked about how it feels to hold your child the first time. Well, at the age of 24 he is a great son and I have held him often. So we felt the love and wanted so much to spend time with him, but we were concerned about communicating with him. Which, when you think about it, that is really strange coming from two people who communicate for a career and teach others how to communicate.

After lunch was over and on the drive home, my wife and I both realized what it was that made communication so difficult with them. They never asked questions. They never asked about us. Even knowing that my wife and I have had many changes in our lives since we had seen them last, neither one of them never asked.

A few days later I needed to be both a coach and a parent to him. I used the phrase, "let me be transparent with you." Now, I'm not sure if he understood how dramatically that this one simple and important technique could help him. But if I want to help him Make a Difference, I had to at least pass it forward. I hope all of you truly understand how simple the process can be, yet how important it is, just to ask questions about people that you are having a conversation with and truly listen to their answers.

It does not do any good if you ask the question and then check out. People can tell when you are genuinely paying attention to them or not. You need to be "present" in the conversation. This also takes effort. It takes concentration. You cannot be thinking about the next question you want to ask. You cannot be thinking about what you plan to do after the meeting or after the party. You need to look the person in their eyes while they are talking and let them know that you are not only listening but that you care.

I have met some extremely successful business people who make you feel you are the only one in the room when you are talking to them, even though you could be one of a thousand. That is a character trait that builds relationships and loyalty. Remember, people don't care how much you know until they know how much you care.

What type of questions do you ask? Are you at a party and was just introduced to someone new? Are you in a business meeting and was just introduced to a CEO of the company you work for or are you the person attempting to sell to that CEO and his company? Are you meeting a potential client for the first time in your office or at their home or even on the phone? Each of these will determine what types of questions to ask. None would be the same.

So, lets see if I can offer some guidance to you that will offer a track to run on when it comes to asking questions. This is important and you need to become proficient because it is the beginning to all relationships.

Remembering that people like to talk about themselves. You should have a mental list of topics that will help you get to know the person. Not their business, not their finances, not anything to do with business, but the person themselves. Things like, family, hobbies, and career. Look at the room you are in or anything in their environment that would offer you an indication of what their interests are. Pictures, trophies, statues, or anything that would point to a sport, hobby, or interest that they have. Once you become good at this, it is much easier to ask the right questions. Even what type of car they drive can sometimes direct your questions. You should become observant in this way because it does help so much.

This will be easy or tough depending on where you meet them. In their office, fairly easy. In their home, really easy, but in a neutral area such as a conference room, hotel lobby, or at a Starbucks is more of a challenge. I meet many people for the first time over the phone since I work with many people across the country. The phone is probably the toughest because you know nothing about them. When planning to meet someone, consider where you will be meeting them and then take the time to prepare your questions. I promise it will payoff if you ask the right ones.

Remember it is also important to put the best smile on your face. Not fake, but genuine. If you are in a bad mood or do not want to be where you are at that specific time, then either make sure your self discipline kicks in and you rise to the occasion or don't meet with them. Remember I said earlier in this book, when motivation leaves you, that is when self discipline needs to kick in.

If you want to ask about something personal, make sure you feel you have the right to ask. If you meet someone for business, don't start by asking if they are married. Especially if you are the opposite gender of the person, this could open up a misunderstanding immediately. So, when it comes to personal questions, what is appropriate? I like to look around the room immediately and see if there is something I can comment on. I also like to genuinely compliment them whenever possible. Must be genuine though. Then I begin by asking them about the topic that you are there to discuss with them. Not many people in today's world want to have their time wasted, so get to the point, but do it gradually.

This is not difficult but it does take practice. I practice this all of the time as I meet people at the car wash or any other place that I can say hi to people. I am not an outgoing person, but I am always working outside of my comfort zone because that is the way we become the best that we can be. So this will be easy for some of you and difficult for others.

Begin by talking about the subject that you are meeting for all the while asking questions that will build a relationship. What interest them the most about...? What have they done in the past? What are they currently doing to find a solution? As you ask these questions do not sound like someone giving them a quiz. Listen in between and make short and observant type comments. After you get some information about what they are looking for, this is a good time to ask about them as an individual. I like to say, "what do you do for fun?" Hopefully this will open up a hobby topic. This will also, at least usually, bring in the family, especially if they are truly a family person.

This is where it is important for you to be somewhat well rounded in your knowledge. But...if you do not know anything about the topic, don't try to act like you do. This will do damage beyond repair if you do that. You will loose their trust before you begin.

It is better to admit that you have never had that pressure or something like that but just admit that you have not done that. I have done many things in my life, but for example, I have never jumped out of a perfectly good airplane. Some people call this skydiving. In the military I jump out of a helicopter but not with a parachute so I cannot relate to that. Obviously there are many other things that I cannot relate to so all of us have sports, hobbies, or situations that we will just listen to. I also say, "tell me more about that. It sounds so interesting." Or so fun, or whatever will fit in the conversation. Remember, people like to be liked and complimented and felt special...but it has to be genuine.

Some of the topics to ask questions should be family, career, hobbies, and travel. Work on questions that will be appropriate in the appropriate settings. Work all of this into your purpose for meeting them and what you want to learn from them in order to be able to help them. If you truly have the mindset to help them, this will come across by the questions you ask. So take this seriously and work at using this to Make a Difference.

Now you have started your relationship by asking the right questions and listening to them attentively. What is next?

I have met a few people recently in business that have an issue with going into what they call, "the friend zone." I find this... well, interesting to say the least. I personally do not have an issue with a business partner, business client, or any relationship going into the friend zone. As long as you stay professional, either it be casual professional which in today's world work best in most places, or if you are at a high level in the corporate world, especially internationally, it is important to keep it professional in your tone of the relationship. Just maintain the boundaries in your relationship.

This is also where communication comes into play. If you are the supervisor or "boss" so to speak, just let it be known, that you need to make business decisions and that your relationship with them while at the office or in the work environment needs to be different than when on your boat or out with family. If this can be done, it is helpful to be transparent, although it is difficult. That is why I brought this one up first.

A supervisor or boss type of a relationship causes a challenge to be friends with the people on your staff or under your supervision. I can only suggest you try it if this becomes a situation you find yourself in. Be transparent and be open with the person that you are building a friendship with. My first suggestion would be not to get too friendly with someone that is under your management or employment. Too many issues could come up in the future that could cause pain to one or both of you. But…you can still build a caring relationship. Just be sure to have boundaries.

Most of all, be fair and consistent in your dealing with everyone. People can see favoritism a mile away. They are already looking for it most of the time, so don't feed their desire to have an excuse on why someone else is moving up quicker than they are.

I know this from personal experience in a couple areas of my life. The first time was while in the Army. I started out at the bottom like everyone else. Even though I had two years of ROTC in college, I decided to go in as an enlisted person, not an officer. Although I felt while I was in there I might as well do a good job, and due to many reasons, I was promoted much quicker than others, even others that were in longer than I was. After a few years I was put in a position of responsibility and authority. I asked the Commander who promoted me how I would hold the position over people who had been in much longer than I had been. His answer was short and simple. "It is only a problem if you let it become one." I paid attention to that but still tried to maintain somewhat of a relationship with a few. I allowed them to call me by my name and not First Sergeant like they should have. There are even nick names in the Army for the First Sergeant, such as "Top" because the First Sergeant is the Top Sergeant of all of the Enlisted men and women.

It did not take long for me to see how that little lapse in protocol was costly to me and to them. I had to pull the friends aside and be transparent with them. Explain that while we were in uniform, the protocol would need to be followed. This was not for me but for the position and for an example of many others to follow. Everyone of them understood and there was never an issue after that conversation. I was lucky.

Some people that I have talked to have had a difficult time making that transition. If you find yourself in this position, think about it, ask questions to people who have come before you. Then, have that conversation and be strong and make sure that you let the people who you are talking to know that this is not up for discussion but this is the way it is. A strong leader needs to be predictable. If you work on being that and being fair with all, everything should fall into place. I will say, however, that this is the toughest challenge when building relationships.

Most of you will not find yourself in a management or leadership role that would cause you this challenge. Therefore, let's talk about building a relationship with a client/customer or someone you want to do business with. Keep in mind all I have mentioned so far and now, open your mind up and do one important task. Remember, we mentioned the golden rule. Treat others as you would like to be treated. Now think about how you would like to be talked to. How you would like to be treated. All of this is important and all of this will allow you to begin the appropriate relationship with the person whom you are with.

Asking the right questions and then listening. It sounds so simple but as you will learn as you attempt to tackle this task, it is not simple. We want to jump in and say something at the wrong time. We may not be "present" while the person is talking. We may want to talk more about ourselves and our experiences than listen.

There are many other challenges you will face as you work on this important characteristic. I promise you all of the effort and hard work will payoff once you truly build that sought after relationship with your client or customer to the point where they will now listen to what you have to tell them and trust that you have their best interest in mind. Now you begin to Make a Difference with people who want to Make a Difference.

Do you do more talking or listening during a conversation? Give three examples of either.

*Have you ever interrupted people while they are talking because you want to finish their sentences? Or have you refrained from interrupting even when you may have wanted to "help" the person? If so, give examples and what the results were.

*Do you try to correct people when they say something that you believe to be incorrect...but you might not have all of the facts?

On a scale of 1 to 10, how would you rate your listening skills?

Conclusion

Alright. Now you know what a Burning Desire is and how much difference it can do to help you accomplish your goals and have your dreams become reality. As I mentioned early on, many people have goals, but actually accomplishing them is another story. It is time for you to take action. Write down each and every question that you found at the end of each chapter. Answer each one after much thought and begin your journey with an attitude that will take each question and each answer seriously. You can only develop the type of success you are searching for if you consider each and every principal that I discussed and put them into action. You will need to stretch yourself. You will need to think outside the box to find whatever you need to do so you can create your Burning Desire. Unless your want becomes a Burning Desire, it will always be just out of your reach. I do not want you to have regrets or live in frustration. My hope is you will take the actions I have lined out in this book and experience the satisfaction and fulfillment you long for. If you commit to taking action, then you will begin the growth that you need to build your dreams into goals and your goals into reality. Become that Difference Maker.

It is my wish that many of you will become the best you can be. Not just for your business, your work, or anything related to making money, but for your loved ones, and for you. It is my sincere wish that those who I come in contact with will be able to say they walked away better for what I was able to give in their lives.

Writing this has been a challenge. I started this because I genuinely believe God has given me a gift – the gift to motivate people to take action. Now it is up to you to take this gift and pass it on. Share this book, and definitely and most importantly, live the gift I have given you. Wake up every morning with a smile because you know you have what it takes and the tools to truly, Make a Difference. Go Do It!!!

Printed in the United States
By Bookmasters